NOW
AND
BEYOND

KENNETH A. SCHOENDORF

Copyright @2021 by KENNETH A. SCHOENDORF

All rights reserved. No part of this book may be reproduced in any form or by any electronic or mechanical means, including information storage and retrieval systems, without permission in writing from the publisher, except by reviewers, who may quote brief passages in a review.

This publication contains the opinions and ideas of its author. It is intended to provide helpful and informative material on the subjects addressed in the publication. The author and publisher specifically disclaim all responsibility for any liability, loss or risk, personal or otherwise, which is incurred as a consequence, directly or indirectly, of the use and application of any of the contents of this book.

WORKBOOK PRESS LLC
187 E Warm Springs Rd,
Suite B285, Las Vegas, NV 89119, USA

Website: https://workbookpress.com/
Hotline: 1-888-818-4856
Email: admin@workbookpress.com

Ordering Information:
Quantity sales. Special discounts are available on quantity purchases by corporations, associations, and others. For details, contact the publisher at the address above.

ISBN-13: 978-1-956017-83-0 (Paperback Version)
          978-1-956017-84-7 (Digital Version)

REV. DATE: 21.11.2021

About the Author

I was born in Louisiana, then became a Vietnam Vet. Afterwards, I worked offshore to oil drilling rigs, close to two decades. I owned an 18-Wheeler hauling freight cross country for over two decades.

My mother is a daughter of a Chief of the Cajun Indian Tribe. She was peaceful and natural, easy to give comfort and attuned to nature. My father was fortunate enough to escape, with the help of his grandparents from Germany, during the rule and reign of Hitler, although he was forced to be in The Hitler's Children Movement as being a pure Aryan blood. He is of goodness and stern in character, came to America and turned into a genuine cowboy, traveling the rodeo circuits. He got here in 1933 and stayed in New York City for a short while. As a boy, he worked the land with Clydesdale horses upon his grandparents' land. After arriving here in America, he saw in a newspaper of hayrides in Louisiana. He thought that, where there is hay, there would be horses. Thus, the reason why he went there and met my mother eventually. She is still alive being younger than my father.

I was raised to respect all people and appreciate the blessings of this earth's creation. Also, I appreciate being able to live in a country that in its Constitution was the right to freedom, and never break the spirit of any animal or person.

I learned respect is given and only taken away if another doesn't deserve this privilege.

Words of my father, even though he called me a Wanderer, were that if a person didn't have principles, morals and honor, then that person was to be Leary of, and they were as a tumbleweed being driven in any direction by the wind.

Table of Contents

A Feeling Known 11
Born to Love 12
Love's Me Love's Me Not 13
Question 14
Future Cry's 15
Continuances 16
Submitting 17
A Realm Enticed 18
Appreciation 19
Balance 20
Become 21
Genuine 22
Gifts 23
Here and Back too Unlimited 24
Blessed 25
Another Teacher 26
Play as a child 27
Peace In You 28
More than Eyes See 29
Wallpaper 30
Wisdom's Search 31
Refried Thinking 32
Awareness Capabilities 33
NOW and THEN 34
Help Wanted 35
Decisions 36
Living 37
Giving 38
Concepts 39
In General 40
Let it Ride 41
Searching 42

House	43
Necessities in Both	44
Rain	45
Unkown Feelings	46
We are Born through Her	47
Passion	48
Love's Unsung Melody	49
Tenderness	50
The Kiss	51
Candle of Love	52
Wonderments Keys	53
Hold On	54
Committed	55
Free as the Wind	56
Devotion	57
You	58
Marvelous You have Enhanced	59
Catch My Eyes-Fill My Heart-Liven My Soul-Luz Estella	60
My Sweet Woman	61
Love in Me	63
Luz Estella	64
Passion River	65
You would think Magical Hat	66
Hopes	67
I am Sorry	68
Page One	69
Rhythm for the Soul	70
Wake Up	71
A Star inside of You	72
Heart and Soul	73
Of You	74
Reserved	75
To Thinking Too Feeling	76
Poetry	77
Prognostacation	78

Eased Intentions Unlimited	79
Mingled Acquaintance	80
Unleashed	81
Painted Idea's	82
Playgrounds & Disciplines	83
Reality	84
The World that Is not	85
In You	86
Progress	87
Seeds Planted	88
Survival's Friend	89
Pondering	90
Passageways	91
Mine or Yours	92
Inspirations of Play	93
Universal	94
Entity	95
One Plus Two Equals	96
Twilight Zone's Nonfiction	97
Nonfictions	98
Willpower	99
Why	100
What Happened	101
Tuning Knobs Inwardly	102
Ways	103
Fused Confusion and Non	104
Negligence	105
Life Abused	106
Rightfully So	107
Wishing	108
Soul	109
Play as a Child	110

This book is dedicated to all the people who care about life.
Including all living things, and giving the respects due.
The willingness to live their beliefs by portraying this in their life.
These are the people that I learn from.

Author's Page

As to everyone who is considerate in compassions to living, I also am one of you.

The ideals and thoughts, realizations being sincere with appreciations for all life are virtues that shouldn't be ignored or forgotten. I have wishes that I too would have more control of angers, impatience to ones breaking my tolerance. I do think that this modern age is of much greatness but never changes the truth.

Somehow confusion generates losing this picture with societies and enterprise. I believe most people all over this earth are born to love and believe in freedoms. A shame our social levels, some overzealous Capitalism individuals and worse yet of Marxism or the government's that want to rule people. Even some cultures hinder along with the bad of jealousies. Common heritages in people are to smile and laugh.

So, we are living and dealing with the shallow neglected concerns of some people.

As the old saying, the rotten apple in the barrel can spoil the bunch is as well with the idea that the bad always ruin spoiling it for the good. Not corrections of this just keeps a good situation gone bad.

So here we are in this life.

Coping and clinging to the company of friends and people that are good.

Prelude

A movie in a perfect story capturing all your attention

A painting that springs as a portrait casting beautiful thoughts in your mind

Sights and sounds merging harmonies to that in your own imagination

Ideas and ideals positively forming

Realizing that goodness creates a happier more

Unlike things that are lesser turning cynical in other directions

Why qualities kept and upheld, guarded in intelligence

Two levels at least when dealing with society and you

For Civilization and Nature combining two differences

Prenominal is the fact your mind and heart do the same

Almost juggling in a circus tossing around ideas holding emotions for better

Earth's Creation miracouisly instills science, philosophies trying for figuring it out

We possess as much as the universe in our minds yet a humbleness of concern

Love of thought, goodness to give or the gift for and of In Love

Playfully as sparrows portraying happiness like children in glee, we live all grown up

Goodness inspires true wit alive in your mood and mind, awakening your heart

Smiling while thinking, awaiting laughter's feel

Most know Bad's not worthy of truth nor fun or in happiness

Laughter will share goodness, shares parts of happiness not downward spirals of cynical

A search for love starts happiness then for the One too share Love in the Two of YOU

A Feeling Known

To tell of love

The feeling most known

Finding and keeping is so new for anyone

Loving more compassionately not just the joys

Makes you feel second for your love of someone

During moments while looking into their eyes What do you do- How do you portray~

Love genuine in your heart

A chance taken laying out your soul giving of your dreams, listening to theirs

Oftentimes wishing you never started

For love an answer to yours in happiness

Pain will weep. . . Realizing your love may go unanswered

They are not ready or want for what you offer

Then the time becomes for love to go self-nurtured

Remembering having loved is much better than not at all

Keep love within alive, sheltered as the entire world is waiting

Not the Lone Ranger Is this only to you

Someone else has been there too

Love takes time finding its' answer

A broken heart is better than to have loved never

Born to Love

A portrait of love is the beauty seen.
Awed inspired even pleasing allure.
Eyes filling minds in lovely ideas.
From sensational to simplicities and all in-between.
Stirring alive many emotions within.
Born of souls from cries at birth.
Love's need is so close easily compared to the breath you breathe.
Joys even sadness
No matter, you learn changes to make.
Without love you are just alone.
Love of life has good concepts.
Love of heart awakens your soul.
Fading loneliness allowing opened never-ending rivers
Living and dying for another in happiness
Nature blooming as the sun adorns
Laying dews or rains replenishing
Night's serenity glowing in moonlit starry skies
Cycles since the beginning of time
Earth is love's picture of teachings
In us emotions and intelligence for fulfilling them

Love's Me Love's Me Not

The petals of flowers fall hoping for a magical answer
Hopes igniting dreams dreamt
Suddenly you are alone in solemn array
Living and dying as if too much for a soul to bear…
Loves' meaning's more intense than life
Capabilities in feelings with those fairy- tale enchantment's
Needing a shared love capturing a heavenly feeling
Portrayed freedoms of Dove's symbol for peace
Filled with desires for beauty's hope looking up to the sky…
Giving like the wind's breeze refreshing and true
Stabilities given feeling safe in these secured dreams
Though excuses you have laid paths for retreating
Knowing without your love existence seems menial
Holding onto reality understanding of lonely and cold
Strengthening though losing dreams
Those petals of flowers fallen to the ground
Lay all the hopes of yours in happiness
So easily imagined being love's content
Sculptured dreams creating at your will

Question

Why must the feelings of love in times makes a joys' sadness
They run deep making you burn
Burn in passions yet burning in pains.
Holding love close flows endearments granted
Ways to live~ feeling dreams~ flying on its' wings.
But the thought of them gone...
Will not deplete tenderness in a heart's yearning to the soul.
Living in the ways of good or fun...
Would be easier so fancy free
The flames of passion could not be as high...
Then again, your soul would not sink as low.
The question of love a ~ magical one...
Feelings in happiness that in times rains in tears.
Nothing is more than this love that you will feel...
Not even you as feeling second, you will become
Nothing is better than knowing, learning, and having love
Only your spirit will know when it arrives...
Oh! What passions in joys of the lessons you will learn

Future Cry's

I used to be so happy all wrapped in you
Living so sweetly thinking the angels did sing
Seemingly floating on petals of flowers from heaven
We were in love as brightly as the sun
Tender was our hearts like gentle rains
Passionate with lusts like torrential floods
You left leaving only this beautiful world
Darling it's so empty without your touch
Raindrops seem dry
The sun I don't notice its' shine
But in the night the stars twinkling bright
The angels must be singing
You're in heaven having me wanting in its' door
Loving seems distant for you're not of this world
You have left behind living still going
Passions like season's flames burning
The memories of you are my living sunrise
Now the sunsets' wishing me beauty in another night
I close my eyes whispering love for you
Tomorrow's hope for love once again brings an angel such as you.

Continuances

Got myself up this morning
Headed over by the mirror hoping to see
I were still there
Hard to tell as feelings do not feel quite right anymore
Lost at love so many times just checking if I am still there
Looking outside the beauties all around I still see
Everything wonderfully pretty in feelings for its' flight
Loves' growing desires still yearning deep in my soul
The spirit of love so quietly whispering
Love's gifts from birth pauses but never dying
Reasons for meanings these learned passions to love
Turning away from my mirror, I think
Tears can express the hope of hugging God's face
No more feelings of losing love as its' been created to see
Nature growing so lovely its' magic for your heart to sing
Turning my eyes towards heaven amazed at its' infinite realms
Seeing infinite beauty from the sky to the ground
Bestowing enlightening hopes through too your soul
Love being as pretty filled in wonderful feelings and thoughts
Has you feeling on Angels' Wings.

Submitting

Did you ever think alone would be easier?

Without the sentimental versions to loving

Within all of yourself lay life's passions

Possibilities to feel, think everything you could ever experience

No vulnerabilities exposed becoming open for wounds

Of your mind's capability knowing all that is thought or felt

In these moments you will realize love

Sharing tenderness growing closer together where trust abounds

Within your soul your heart wants sharing in all this

Yet to make a relationship last is not so easy

Inside every person lay stored dreams, of love, hopes or fears

Treasures of cherished feelings

Unique individualism so blessed we are to have

Here lay some problems with love for giving or letting in

Sheltered as sacred from showing feelings as some live just physical or intelligent

Maybe protected in a shroud of ways with humored ideas on living

Love's vastness being so much as the prettiness and volume to this world

Learning of love even learning its' growth although not knowing exactly how

Understanding those feelings of love granting attentions needed

The giving of hearts and souls too and for each other's mind

A Realm Enticed

Twilight's comfort in eased array
Softly hued across the horizon
Sky light of blue and orange in purplish pinks
Colorfully outlined against the sky
Inflections of heaven assimilate too your mind
The stars at night enchanting souls
Moonlight glows romancing hearts
In your eyes this night's sweet bliss
Silhouette's dancing filling your thoughts
Being able to touch as remarkable as this
Enticingly moods enhanced alive
Physical desires tasting sensualities' passions' lust
Sweet tenderness~ savored~ rising exotically
Time and space and love in your arms
Nature reveals Her intent of the night
She so painted it mysteriously mystically romantic
Conjuring in you desires created
Touching in kisses releasing her energy
Splendors dawned magnificently in pleasures
A night's sweet erogenous romantic endeavors

Appreciation

Earth rotating as you yawn… Brushing of hair ~ rubbing sleep from your eyes

A sweet baby cries in fragile needs.

Headline news of things gone wrong… or a life stopped.

And you breathe, ready for another day.

Breezy, flowing winds or still…

Sunlight or rain pouring down…

Thoughts along with laughter…

Sometimes in feelings of dismay for bearing…

Moments hoped for play or bringing comfort in life to share.

Quick glances over a horizon in a thought…

You know of blessings meant for life…

Time for learning through today though more from yesterday.

Like a baby's birth is of a new beginning…

Frangible delicate gifts in life of purity and innocence.

Let that be of your soul for thriving within your heart…

Allowing growth becoming passionate granting compassion to excel

Tear's shed even shared amongst ideas of beauty…

Keeps the warmth of humanity… Your tomorrows much sweeter.

Balance

A baby growing so content in playing
Smoothly until the word... No! Enters their world
Confusion sprouts if an opinionated or self-serving
How great if it is protecting that child's world
A child's innocence never to be exploited by society's views
Life goes on and growth becomes apparent
How strange awareness lingers thinking of you then of others
Now a maze of restraints is cast as you wonder
These can be of good, yet some will lose attainment
Often puzzlement looms
Which path of yours or theirs
Nice if from birth Courtesy and Respect were bestowed
A no can be as accepted as a yes
Different views easily thought if harmony is of you
Your soul has memories of innocence pure in its' concern
Now that you have grown confusion generates many fold
So many other's ways with thoughts to consider
Funny how you become of others
Wonderful how you can disregard lost reasoning
Still confusion lingers in choices spun relentlessly
Watching-listening-learning from within and of others

Become

You can take a book in the reading its contents
Not knowing what is within, learning anew
Stories of intrigue, romance, mysteries, of fictional or non
Many ideas, many knowledges gained
Things aiding for intelligence and of your ways
Feelings possessing passions marvelous for anyone
Somehow emotional characterizations taunt losing its' hold
Fears of another's thought can ridicule opening your heart's soul
Thoughts that you are the only one to feel as such
Embarrassment's vulnerability's something you opened yourself unto
Seems safer keeping inside although it lingers in lonely solitude
Easy being some of yourself embracing other factual conjectures to everyone
Those pretty thoughts feel seemly fairy-tale dreams anyway, you think
Slowly those feelings inside you become cold of non-believing
Confusing losing your reality for truths are such as you in your soul
Ideas the other part of living, feelings are such as you
Be of courage for your heart in finding moments sharing
Look to the things around you of this Heaven and Earth
You cannot tell me, that they do not make you feel
Reasons planted, created if you will, in your soul to become

Genuine

Raindrops from above
Quenching thirsts below
Savoring life's desires abundantly
Walking merrily in blessings granted
Thorned paths to be neglected
Horizons of beauty made for optimistic
Shallow thoughts are as too the well empty of water
Simplicity covers the vastness of sky and oceans
Extravagance is timely spent in vivid illusions
Elegance is a grace well praised
Stylish adheres by chosen directions at will
Truth never falters remaining the same
You mirror the reflections of decisions
Be in concern for earthly blessings
Paths of unique should be genuinely sought
Simplicity in elegance formed from sweet grace
With an awe of beliefs too steadfast paths for truth
As the heavens glow from the moon across this land
Worldly matters have not been as grand
Be wise in decisions one day the last one made

Gifts

Hunger's light shines wants for desires
This idea enlivens imagination
Thirsts seeking to quench
Endeavors you search for pleasures' adventures
Sharing becomes replaced due to some passions
Enlightenment is enough realizing companions make better
Backdrops from life spawned, thoughts
Sights so amazing your wishes to comply
To be of what is felt lined with conversations
Excitement rushing thrilling the mind
Activities physical or mental
Either pleases all senses
The thoughts born in visions enticingly of beauty
Uncanny the tangibility brought to life
The art in making creations come alive
At will, your achievement
So fortunate with eyes to see
Hearts to feel - Minds to think
Human traits of passions spontaneously allured
To live as genuine this earth so impassioned

Here and Back too Unlimited

Optimism-pessimism, oh what views!

These things lead frontiers in the aspects of thinking

Back again even all around yet never changing

Endless time consumed discussions but opinions never faltered

Wondering if some minds only fixate in one maybe two dimensional

Losing the big picture like chess or facts that can fill a chest

Barge's untied drifting lost amidst currents

People talk without really thinking

Fantastic if imaginary or fun-filled with laughter

But certain things need contemplation's expertise to ponder

Frustrating caught in singular dimensional conversation

Every fence has two sides if people could only remember

Thinking would start at two maybe elevating into three dimensional

Their mind fully functioning calculating every angle, full circle

Opinionated ceasing laid by the wayside as if a favorite color

Intelligence would increase as many views could be covered

Understanding might be able finding common ground

Arguments easily discussed without the conclusion of winning

Sessions too learn in talking eliminating egotistical moods

Thoughts or ideas genuinely debated leads to truths for many

Blessed

I was thinking about you and others

How I am one of life's living on this earth

Many species granted gifts with food and air to breathe

Small thoughts but important of the soil and rock as every affect has an effect

The dimensions to life just might be more than what we see

Perfectly explained by gazing at all the beauty seen

As extra amenities optional gathering of lovely harmony in our mind

Rain-sunshine-waterfall-forests bestowing beauty for hearts, minds and soul

Individual thoughts or feelings even being able to do this reading

Creations such a magic in this word even this earth before us lays

How things of opposite make paths for realization, nature and civilizations

Passageways guiding to truths

You've lived long enough to learn and know

Things usually don't apparently exist for nothing

Yet we were given this phenomenal of earth and life for free

This gift to live is so much a blessing

You can talk-think and feel- did you wonder what got and keeps this going?

A miraculous part that there's more than you know to what makes you live

Not just the fundamentals of blood, heart and brain with all its' accessories

But the spirit of life given letting you become

Another Teacher

Oh, mighty oceans of vastness seemingly ever reaching

So imaginative teaching joys and scares

Covered by the skies hidden deep within your treasures

Mysterious is your essence covering three quarters of earth

Drawing moisture too clouds by your partner the sun

Ponds and lakes you gave of saturation's

All waters you possess

Giving the living of life feeding rivers with rain continuing your search

Making for land you cover its' vastness quenching its' thirst

Reflections for infinite enchantment by the moon's glow

Uninterrupted space between you and the sky

Even the stars contribute to your beauty

Many tales of your fury yet everyone and things have need of you

How you made portraits of splendor for our memories

Whether of backdrops for boating in fun - swimming or divers

Fishermen fishing for food even the birds dive in

Your sides of good or bad still retain balances for everyone

The teachings of respects for you hold many scary creatures

Through it all spawning many passions- mystically mental or physical

Without you ~ My Mighty Friend ~ this world hasn't any wonders.

Play as a Child

Emotionally drained intellectually spent
Silence fought but never defeated
Overwhelmed with feelings where thoughts abound
Grasped by this vastness of life
Of livings' maze searching for paths or glimpses of light
Its' shine for joy of thinking to smile
Like clouds floating, creating somber yet enchanted dreams
So, of darker ones give mystical gloom
Caught in whirlwinds of passions
Intensity of desires beckoning yet not ringing
Lost where moments feel become dark
Dulled senses trying to take their flight
Remembrances of heart's soul seeking happiness
But the mind hesitates to see all reality's intersections too thoughts and feelings
Crazy desperate funny clichés of captains and kings
Winning knowing losing is a part too
Struggles at times keeping your shine
Without a mind and heart, a soul never shows to see knowing its' truths

Peace In You

Retrieving so much beauty before you seen
Passing through your heart in tenderness
Lodging deep within the soul
Later for quieter days or ones in dismay
Sweet feelings bestowed of that beauty for your soul
Acting as a life buoy saving thoughts granting harmony
As a balancer for the sorting out bad for better
Ones of lesser quality discarded from your mind
Your soul so happy in the decisions that you made
A heart freer in more room for compassion
Love blossoms unlimited and in boundaries dear to hold
Having love so strong that hate holds no ground
It could be even said without love~ no beauty is felt
Most everything love can touch even change
Thoughts seem and can be so perfect
Living them is not so easy
Open channels for your heart of souls
Thinking in understanding yet never forgetting feelings
Courtesy such a sweet guide ever so appreciated
Once started this in you ~ never will you quit

More than the Eyes see

Feelings of beauty thoughts in purity
Unbounded and diversity soaring
Compassion not to be chained
Living in freedom not selfish ways
Beginning of time these things never changed
Once not so complicated until populations grew
Materialistic quick fixes soon became abundant
Reasons for convenience casting not guidance jeopardizing of morals
Where the paths of truth got paved aside for society measures
Like a fix of addiction that thirst abounded
Solutions possible ~ remembering materialistic fades
Nothing more apparent though than for search of a happiness
Purity and truths or beauty enlivens peace
Passions of physical too compassions of soul
Desires to be thrilled or the ones too give
Ever seeking the ultimate harmony being content and complete
Acknowledgment of scholars' artists and priests
Back to the child who lives in innocence
Hopes for all to know that life is more than fame or gold

Wallpaper

I sit amidst my inner self amongst life and time

Views of this world all their cultures laid before my eyes

We know of reality's function the social of society plays

As furniture we have become unless friends indoctrinate

Pain, laughter, love, survival we know outside that time made us ice

Cold to indifference anonymous we ignore not of our interest

One nicer part of living always are exceptions to the rule

Some give acknowledgment just by a glimmer of an eye

Keeping sacred to the better half of living

If gardens were our cities, being cultivated as forests in tranquility

We could be growing radiating many pleasantries

Exclusion of medical, science from these wonders, is modernism better

Obligating the essences of humanity for materialistic structure

Traps the nature order or innocence as progress thought sculptured better

Comparisons left to preferences

Is it better to feel harmonious or better in feeling metropolitan?

Yes, the two are of varieties we have in the life of living

At our whims we can be of and do whatever we choose

Perceptions are the focal point realizing not to lose humanities

Like a deck of cards~ dreams are there~ lesser can be dealt or discarded

Wisdom's Search

To those who are swimming in the sea of life
Cherishing of its' treasures
Living and playing vibrantly in spirited fun's essence
Inspired in compassion with passion for living
Lay all those realities for living dreams
Most of us in being the audience fewer being the stars
Similar for completeness without any two appreciation's concepts sparkle less
Brings into focus of venturing out
Intellectual spawns' ideas but spoils a party
Humility lacks enthusiasm
Words hopefully create truths in meanings
Civilizations culture split-levels of people through societies
Egotistic finds this a place for dwelling
Not to mention the ideologies that are tried, persuaded to follow
Confusion populates spreading turmoil needing law enforcement
The necessities the gentle and peaceful need for protection
Almost unknown why nature's choice the animalistic of bigger eats the smaller
Yet gorgeous horizons exist in heavenly rainbow beauties from a promise long ago
The harmony to learn of good, bad, and still live beautifully, now
Underwritten somewhere life's Creation wakened and one day we all will

Refried Thinking

Expressions felt in the slogans that are made

Things to do with living

Tricky sometimes in comparisons as art for this process of thinking

Simple when things are of glad and good

Not so clear the clarity too sad or bad

Shifting into deciphering feelings from thinking

A juggler we become back and forth

Tossing from logic into emotions

Sanity plus humanity seeking so sweeter a balance

Rationalizing as a scientist then the mentor

Looking for conclusions in that of harmony's peace

Confusion might cluster giving none for specific directions

Surrounded amongst the problem you face

Troublesome or painful yet weary of the multiple options

Positions cluttered until walked away

Like the very young with their belongings tied to a stick

Sometimes just seeing the picture in you realizing what will be missed

Missing or lacking insight builds webs of confusion

Anything with too many holes floating won't be so easy

Living has its' burdens but waiting and thinking sets you free

Awareness Capabilities

You ever meet people who say they are open-minded
Finding they are hardheaded in their own
A kind of respect is born yet possibly disregard
Beliefs are hard to shake or even change
Unique individualism a blessing and a curse
Depending upon circumstances or you determine its' growth
Acceptance or cast-off is decisions you must make
Valued morals and social freedoms intelligently pondered
Responsibilities for an open-minded person
The unique in each other will field these boundaries
Conclusions why so many thoughts even social levels
A passive person will seem so nice
Yet in times wishing a stand they would take
Same of the one leading the way
A back seat is nice to see if they can patiently fit
Aware of surroundings' and of others' thoughts
Enlightens becoming more
Learning changes if a positive gain
Positions understanding becoming more versatile
Seriously speaking, something we could all afford

NOW and THEN

Think of now and then -in specific- way back then

Times of ages of history so long ago

How lives were spent without technologies

Moments spent dwelling or conjuring though developing amazing capability

Sources tapped as if from Creation itself, said in ancient times

A mind was still as of now for infinite possibilities

Some found magic of the earth's power- filled energies

Not a small feature this earth's phenomenal power

As if diminishing mankind's intensities

Times so fast of now our minds seldom reflects to the past

The days of honor with nobility the inspired words charmed in speech

Gallant and free with enchantment of the beauty that was seen

Souls harmonized in spirit for the romance of life's simplicity

Where men tipped their hats to a lady and proud was their chivalry

More significantly how one's word was to die for in honor

Those rugged times how strange but life looked for the ever-after

Fly in a plane or drive then take a walk~ tell me which has more time

The slower we go with time the more we see to think and feel

Technology is of wonders and so wonderful in our lives

But with not the time to reflect ~ then what are we really doing

Help Wanted

Honorable such an excellent characterization
A virtue to trust in your thoughts you can stand for
Beyond life as even in death ~ honor is had
Alone, it will defeat deceits of integrity or immoral
Like passion it builds desires
As with love even if lost it will cling to your soul
Knowing the best, less is deterioration
Imperfection is chosen when doing this
Cliché's of taking up slack or be doing without
Variations we adjust to smoothly sail
Accommodating we make to gain or for conclusions
Honor is the one that is unchangeable
Like breathing accesses' life, stopped, it will cease living
Honor conceived fills every fiber of living
Invisible life buoy is stopping persuasion if honor within
Whatever circumstance even infidelity's pull
No matter what emotion - ideas or pressure
Temptation's prey anyone yet honor is a giver of direction
Like a tumbleweed blown whichever way of wind
Without honor a tumbling tumbleweed you are

Decisions

Many walks in life, mostly freely we choose
Different feelings for the thoughts that are viewed
But one's chosen path of virtuous and righteousness
Very well considered correct
Opposite this will open subjected paths tainted with deceits
Amongst deceitful souls will never know true happiness
Become of what you know is right, portraying for others to see
The soul of morals genuinely excels in joyful splendors
Rich or poor this truth exists as money being only tangible
Laughter is merely fun thus not completely an article of happiness
Wit is the example of catchy clichés' that make for play and thought
Satisfaction derives from essences given or obtained
Pride is the honor within that consists of very well balanced
Of course, if accepted in these concepts of good let us continue
Confusing why others chose the paths lesser of qualities
Those baffling aspects of living that we all deal with
Excuses tendered for ill performance or lack in upbringing
Even hatred a possibility
Never-the-less alibi's for not clearly thinking
Ignorance the lack of concerns like tipped over trash cans widely polluted

Living

We live our lives sometimes thinking of things to do
Yearning souls' even playfulness for meanings to our lives
Dreaming destiny's flight in hopes of dreams coming true
Feelings' for growing more, thoughts to be wise, learning of desires
Though sometimes inside us we cannot answer
As if in a mystic trance from the sea under infinite stars
Enlightened races through minds thrilled with life
Knowing absolutely this wonderment exists
Still these feelings in words we are driven to find
Wanting of answers for explanations about life
Like a miracle, living portrays so many wonders
Things beyond conscience's comprehension
The feeling of lost subsides accepting this blessing
Some things are not really ours to question
Being of good with the giving in caring
Sharing in blessings for all others living
Smiling with this earth's beauty ceasing worry for every answer
Reflected in oneself in kind ways as proof living can be better
Understanding's peaceful setting assuring stable
As the floating of a feather back down to earth

Giving

Envision a day of sunshine glowing radiantly in thoughts
Frisky energy filling you with play
Necessities like children, life so needs their innocence
Lucky for childhood as we adults soon forget
Big industrial too corporate domains or dominant sales personnel
Worldly matter's wheels' always turning even our defenses'
Disillusioned to a child how money makes the world go round
Locking carefree away in our hearts tackling the almighty dollar
Not so totally are we too fault of this
But a difficult course lay stored for the tender hearted
A juggler of time must we be to keep a balance
Working to obtain always collecting substantial means
Ceasing quality time for those in our lives
All is in vain if losing that time
Don't wait for rain to slow you down
Reign your thoughts for sharing of yourself
Rein in ambitions just to be company with family and friends
Isolate moments as fruitful spending glee
Seriously consider values important in life's meaning
Look at that child-friend-sweetheart also remembering they want you

Concepts

Brought into this world as a babe

After some play quickly came self-discipline

Taught in ways to conform

Understandingly accepted

Through years of schooling in appreciation for education

Then came your thinking rationally in the reality of life

Where knowledges gained educationally merge coherently with living

Applying all that was learned yet not shunning compassion

Still comes the bafflingly understanding of love

Logic and rational know not the heart of emotions

Even sentiments with concerns for others fail in some education

Mathematically or scientifically as love and compassion have not any logic

Yet we process this and much more

What can be decided best if affections state irrational

Confusing is life when it unveils compassion or love

Do, we give of ourselves or sacrifice for the well of another

Sentimentally ~ yes - as love and compassion are giving

Socially or of reality might thwart these ideas and efforts

Which gives to your strength to conquer much soul-searching

Treasures are freedoms for humanity not a socialist indoctrinated agenda

In General

We share most thoughts in the feelings too life only to differ in opinions

Of loves, happiness, fun and play, the intrigues, keeping satisfied.

Unfortunate guides of hate, depression, jealousies burdening too bear.

Choices made in the betterment of our lives...

Still, some are more aware and attuned to this life...

Persecutions we stay in line, knowing truths to die for...

Others who want to be popular or even rule populations

Vanity gets carried away in lusts for power.

Equal of another yet success measured through society, not of truths

Soft, sweet, tenderness so often ignored.

Thoughts of being weak are views from this mad world until we fight

Money reaches even the most intelligent but not the meek.

Fame is an idol but not love of virtues

Starvation or deaths have always been around as true with beauty

Complexities to life so confusing, seeking ultimate ways in being

Without greed, things would be closer to tranquility

So easily spread this cupidity and false idolism

It filled the land.

Not to all does this exist is why life enchants

Truth is heard with hope unfortunately not sought

Lost in mazes of population's opinions and only the beauty is sung.

Let It Ride

What a life with many things at our fingertips to do

Metropolitan's entertainment intriguing or idle pleasure's games

Feeling's fulfillments, seeing beautiful nature

Amazement's astonishments at every bend

Always within our sights touching within

Truths can be merry or sadness to bear even bearing policies forced to follow

They built a world not letting us play or dream too much

Too much work ~ breaking down ~ locking most of our time away

So many boundaries with much stress ~ hard to let freedoms fly

Confusion started living in this world making someone else rich

Now we create like the earth's magic before our eyes

Living in our hearts and of our minds

Obstacles before us we conquered to defeat

Not victims of this world's greed but letting our souls' soar

Grasping at laughter's to be ours ~ adventurously playing

Not forgetting love that sails onto pretty horizons

We can have high spirits when the society is material

Thinking is a flight to freedom overriding things dull or bad

Dismays may be grim but impassioned to live brings back joy

Never to be down but getting back up in riding for life again

Searching

Life sets you aside in its' times
Pausing ~ leaving feelings humble
Moments of a soul awakening beckoning coming alive
Possessing desires happily even solemn appreciation
Emotions felt immensely portraying views of pretty thoughts
With passions you will smile completeness in realms of beauty
Ideas living more fulfilled enriches your mind
Sharing means so much more with those tenderly affections
Living dreams with someone in truth consistently
Passions for love~ intimately of body-soul-heart and mind
Beautiful feelings clinging infinitely alive in dreams
Living intimately wanting occupancy not shallows of emptiness
Desired passions left waiting openly for tenderness to become
Fortunate is the truth of ones having this
Or learn content in solitude of loneliness the beauty isolated within
This questions in pinpoint that life must be searched
Reasons of so many paths multiple directions waiting for decisions
Numerous changes when life leads differently in journeys
But will set you aside making you reflect within and all about
Capturing of your soul in learning finding you long for living

House

When seeing of a house…

Daydreaming about life on the inside…

A heart yearns and a mind wants serenity from the outside

Acknowledgments of closeness even when in strife

Desires in wanting of this life.

Like a haven, storing trust in hopes' growth for the lives sharing

Efforts for love gained raising of a family

Humbled thoughts growing old together with all its' celebrations…

Memories in your soul embracing every endearment.

Learning sharing, giving, or taking, trying to be in harmony…

Passions turning a house into a home, lingers on your heart.

Living in knowing families bring more completions to life.

The knowledge gained in learning how

Holding true, children and parents are meant as a family, together.

Happiness with play and laughter yet stern with good upbringing

Happiness's smiles and tears from the joys and disappointments.

To make a home of this house will soothe all within…

Making a house a loving home is something not everyone will do.

The family in this house, is a love none can take

Necessities in Both

Seriously joking in the realizations of man and woman

Ideally for the other closest to perfect making something better

Good friendship fine companionship yet difference in assumptions

Man's protections of strength, authoritative protection even baritone voice

Comfort's companion of compassion is woman soft in thoughts and her touch

Chromosomes linked yet differ one pair between man and woman

Yet they are notably at times opposite in thinking and habits

Mostly girls playing dolls, cooking, making a home and dressing nice

In general boys conquering, experimental, playing police officers, robbers or doctor

Man looks at woman thinking he has been conquered

Her femininity aft aside his dominance into a calmer tenderness

Without her, he is content in a tough hunter

His strengths learn innovative approaches as she lays new understandings

She has ways getting him thinking love

Beneficial, she feels the security as he holds her

Protection she gains in this world of cruelties

Man and Woman merging harmonies making love even if desired creating children

Together, sensational attributions in sensual and passionate

Any minds more than one calculate factual in different views

So, this saga continues of man and woman

Companions creating wonders yet jokingly of different planets

Rain

A morning of rain subtle with feelings of cozying up
Gentle thoughts, sweet Harmonys' tender warmth's lovely
Livings' mystified mysteries we do notice
The introversion of a mind captures itself
Footloose- fancy free or the soul mate can be pondered
Yet only one seeks eternal of your heart
Deeply inward of souls, a yearning of love
Livings' threshold although spinning in multiple directions
Up front the mind's delightful view desiring simplicity
Hearts' fleeing loneliness
Tenderness resonating throughout your whole being
Living of passions in the soul's glowing embers
Some choices withdrawn will chance freedoms
Pondering thoughts casual or eternal
Levels of intensities and passions to climb
The sun or rain remarkable affects
Playful or cozy in subtlety one needing sheltered comfort
Oh! A morning of rain to slowing you down
Times of quietness leaving contemplation's even for the soul

Unknown Feelings

Knowing that somethings inside going in you

Yet no answers or even questions stir anywhere

No confusion not anything to even think about

Going about living knowing an unknown feeling is on the inside

Checks and balances evolving going through all the routines

Everything seems fine, smiles, balance even sadness' remain intact

Rationalizing using logical thoughts or of wit for spontaneity

Wow! Life sure gives puzzlements in its' times

To that of a little bug that keeps hovering serving as a reminder

Something is going on inside you and no clue of it yet

A day or two who knows how long

You do not feel riled just bewilder

So, of hopes in wanting that little bug turning into a butterfly

At least something pretty comes about

Knowing its' there but clue-less finding out whatever it is

Harmony seems to exist, so this is nice

No problem of anger for this is not what it is about

But most definite, feelings with hollow invisible thoughts stirring inside

Could be the growth to a meaning but soon you will find out.

Life's uncanny but surely interestingly mystique all the while

We are Born through Her

Of all things and thoughts
Imagining infinity or the will to endure
Never ceasing of a mind wandering
Insights of thinking, wished visions to aide splendor's delight
Beauties formed created in the mind compiled of dreams
Adventurous heroic flights or yet remarkably simple
Awed inspirations before our sights this earth, we do see
Humans, another form from this energy of earth
Self-corrected modulating directives we portray
But our intensities seem created
Guided examples she lays before us
We start learning how to be with this life
A teacher she is
Fills minds, hearts, souls the astonishment of lovely she bestows
But most definitely spawns our intellect
Serenity stems from her subtle quietness
Passions erupt too her mighty force
Our endeavors affected by her creations
We are us looking at her mirrored reflections

Passion

Flying... as if on the Wings of an Angel
Soaring... proudly as an Eagle.
Playing... like the Sparrow's daily delight.
Living... the Dove's symbol of Blessed Peace.
Making... Love vibrantly as the Sun's Brilliance.
Sharing... Love's Glow in a Moon's Silhouette.
Giving... a tenderness like the gentle misty rain.
Being... sensual as the Whisper of Love.
Loving... is the picture of a portrait.
Allowing... Us in creating the Art

Love's Unsung Melody

Feel Tears of Joys
Hearts united eternally growing
Sharing between in us every way.
Touching dreams every day.
Passions freed living adding this charm to life…
Sweetness to thrills Living and Making Love
Soaring upon heights, glowing amongst stars
Pure Love at Heaven's door.
Souls unchained in harmony's freedom
Look for truth in your heart not the fears of Heartache.
Striving, giving thoughts showing beauty bestowed of our Hearts
In our eyes we would see Hungers of Love.
Caressed from my touch gentle as a feather across your Skin.
Wild and Sensual expressing melodies
Our Kiss.
Unleashing as smooth yet strong like Waterfalls…
Enchanting, Passionate Desires, Thundering Down.
As Light is to Day, Dark is to the Night
Warmed in Coldest of times, Light in the Darkest Hour, we are not Conflicted
So Simple. To Believe, With Me. The Will of Love.

Tenderness

As the bird's flight is magic on air

My ways soar in delights by you

Where harmonies cooled hungers for passion, I will make it so

Given tenderly and easy for your heart's soul

All the wonders of you my sweet lay in me

Flowing in beauty as earth's blessings

Whether the laughter's of play

Or the deepest meanings in our souls

I will be there sharing yours with me

A simple little daisy flower so wonderful as the rose

They are different looking that is all

I want to be magnificently living this with you

Finding right times inspired beautifully as sunrise and sunset

Blue-sky feelings of white clouds added for our happiness

The rains freshening our love and the storms as we stay not conflicted

Of the vastness of sea's filled charms for unlimited passions our reality

The night sky twinkling so mystically enchanted

I will give along in warm feelings as a moon's silhouette

Glowing from my heart this incredible tenderness for you

The Kiss

Many thrilling passionate things in life finding love
One so fulfilling of magical is the kiss
Not simply the touching of lips though a blessing of wonders
The feelings of passion that are given in many feelings
Of you to them unleashing passions for sharing
From within become you to them so they can see and feel
Tenderness softly warmed of the beautiful thoughts within
Love caresses a kiss from your soul in meanings of them too you
Alive of you both sharing affections those moments made to stand still
Love's harmony is as a river everlastingly flowing
Smooth mirrored images yet Rippling born in the two of you
All the most wonderful sensations ever being felt alive in a kiss
Desires planted in a heart are yours to release
Become of your love inside them with that kiss
Holding so dearly your hands to their face hesitating intimately intense
Kiss with your thoughts for them to understand
Let free of reality's demands portraying of you too their lips
Enchantments of them, your feelings will guide you along
Realms of love sensually forming lusts born in both of you, always

Candle of Love

Remembrances of good caused thrilled emotions
Free Willed spontaneous exertions
Especially for one so special whom lit your heart
Passions flamed your minds even as your bodies touched
Desires pledged forever, together
Memorable moments lived and love was made to stand still
When hearts and bodies merged growing in your souls'
Invisible candles were lit for love
The dawning of something so fresh and new
Some things change yet memories never do
Reminiscing will keep those flames impassioned
Rekindles every desire in affections
A candle lit in this way needs relighting together, watching it flicker
Living is meaningful try being its' portrait
Loving cherishing those fond times times tenderly spent
Souls warmed to the harmony shared
Minds remember as thoughts grow in what the two of you created
Living in this world sharing a life, cherished by the two of you
Remembrance wears smiles and those tears in a life's love deeply shared
Eternal until death do you part as you go about every day

Wonderments' Keys

Learn of Grace of living not just graceful in your style

Infatuation a path to love if carefully trodden

Acknowledging Grace enlightens ease about love

Pondering about the Wonderment of life for understanding answers

For learning this Wonderment finds the enchantment of love

Embracing Grace fills a soul majestically thrilled in solid foundations

Mystically alive genuine uniqueness so real

Look towards heaven allowing Grace for filling your life

See the Wonderment of this earth even from the air that you breathe

Learn how to be… Gazing upon Purity besides just beauty alone

Realizing storms keeps balances of the bad to cherish the good

Spark an infatuation in someone sharing this Wonderment

Live appreciating Grace for it is a given love already gave

Think of the babe's cradle in the innocence of life

Accept as a gift's blessing accepting fulfillment in your heart

You will find joys living, growing utmost never alone

Love is your eternal walk for happiness of its' path already there

More radiantly rich than all the money in the world

If you wonder of the Wonderment all else will fall into place enriched

Hold On

So, you fell in love…
Loving these feelings of glee so charmed
Loneliness faded sailing away on lost winds
Having a life with so much joy
Even visions danced through your head
Songs in your heart give energy to life
Perfect this love… Days through the night…feeling wonders
Time uncontrollable and enviable makes or breaks
Dreams fading in a world eroding perfection
Hearts remaining in passions still alive in a soul
This love blocked yet never depleted
Despaired and wondering of love's dream
Humanity blows selfishly as of its 'sails constricted in a maze
Alas! Living as loving is learning to forgive
Infatuations are harder to retain and remain needing much sharing
Spontaneity might be a new mate refreshing anew
If just romance, you search then igniting is burning a candle
Don't let a sad reality lose too your love deep within
Find out more of love before starting again
Grace saves for it has already been tested, and He won.

Committed

In love ~ laughter's tenderness rings in affections
Silent bells will haunt differences
Struggling keeping sweet the harmonies
Love faces reality
Emotion's strain making for intelligent rebounds
Overlooked just for wanting love
Not so hard if only a few yet deadening if many
Silent scars forming ~ fading it all away
Only intelligence's reasoning holding in place
Shinning all the different auras of love
Don't be confused in learning commitments
Yet be wise in love
Worldly views only widen the gap
In your heart and mind lay answers
Love can be felt untouched
Love can even be stern yet giving but still a no
Blessed with emotions stuck with thinking
Sometimes torn in multiple directions
If being in love is the focus forget opinions go back to wise, a heavenly experience

Free as the Wind

Rolling hills whispering pines, backdrops against the sky

Vibrantly amidst sunny or stormy mystique

Stories and songs, inspiration granted from the beauties of nature

Sweet feelings rhythmic, true with any beat

Picturesque enchantment in awed delights

Nature's imprints our very souls

Forming silently in thoughts guiding passions

Building sensations learnt from storms of howling winds

Loud crashes of thunder, streaks of lightning

She teaches us excitements we turn into ecstasies

How to be of real yet make marvelous

Desires turns into hungers

Thirsts~ becoming apparent in the dreams we search

Burning fevers from within us of passionate

Inspirational thoughts of the mind for beauty yet in passions

As nature filled herself with so many wonders

We too can be another amazement~ making love's sensations

Time standing still as the touch from our bodies

Thrills form our lusts~ sending into each other as sensual finds its' place

Yes, phenomena are in our reach~ passing through us into another

Devotion

People could join too this world's enchantment
Possibilities beyond mystical admiration
Thriving in them this Garden of Eden
From a smile capturing ways of being
Seeking of living, learning how to be
Quests waiting in moments to reflect and love
Intensity flowing or just simply calm
Royalties or as simple flowers down a hillside
Their quality never ceases in my mind
Living lovingly in freedoms with serenity of soul
Capturing as if sunlight radiating energy
Shining directions in living life's joy
Those hearts so tender of helping another out
So inspirational silent melodies
Emotions felt yet thoughts persevered
Nothing out of life good or wholesome goes untouched
Dreams have always been ready to live
Flying in all that is real
You my dear can be a breath for life

You

An artist's brush can do wonders with three-dimensional
If my words to love appear only in the one, believe me.
They are more than a shadow.
Time is endless.
Where at moments they stand still...
Then seem to fly.
Time with you is so alive.
I love time, spent with you.
Gazing upon things that fills a mind visioned in awe
A smile will spring across ones' face.
A heart will be warmed to the beauty
Over the thoughts of something so pure
You do all these things, to my heart.
Enchanted in the Thoughts of You. . .
Mystified over the Beauty of You. . .
Charmed at the Sight of You.
Touching my soul.
Where a longing grows a need of you.
A Passion. . . For without You...
I would have never known Love this way

Marvelous You have Enhanced

Amongst mountain peaks, higher than clouds

Significant sensations inspired from awe

Magical mystics, entrances me unto your beauty

Of your womanly appeal joyful breasts'

From the beauties of your face and eyes come angelic harmonies

So attractive of lovely sweetness is your skin

Serenity's calm ponds encircled by sights and sounds of waterfalls

Cool crisp air like sounded nuance shades of blue

Fills my lungs in warmth's of you in how you live

Graceful and elegantly casting admirations as a princess you move

Simply natural as a Lillies upon waters

Impressions overwhelmed in me the marvelous of you

Treasures beyond glittering diamonds or pearls, silver, and gold

Priceless your beauty capturing all nature's splendor

Energies of sensual forthcoming radiating boldly enveloping of soft

Temperature's risen desirous, passions ignited

As rains quenching thirsts moistures remain upon your lips

Horizons of artistry beckoning desires even a portrait

Enchantments of a woman to a man, enticing in every essence

Words distract your beauty as you are breathtaking upon any pedestal

Catch My Eyes - Fill My Heart - Liven My Soul - Luz Estella

I look at your face My love My Sweet Amor
Only pleasantries of the loveliness you are
Deep inside me stirring love within
Living inspirations - touch's igniting
Meanings of life's reasons
The flower's destiny expressing beauty
A forest's intensities listing life's wonders
Enchanted gifts for living
You in flesh possess these sensations
Majestic mountains views dipping into valleys below
Skyline's border following a river's flow
Portraits for my heart sketched by you
Mystic allures of neon excitement's you fill
City street's wildness with nested restaurants
Energy's dance floor a life of celebrative ways
Colorful fashions as you sit amongst high rises'
Thrilling to be by your side
Your tenderness waiting for moments to make
Sensuality's feathers or volcanic eruptions
The natural you cast in extravaganza's dye

My Sweet Woman

You make me so happy ~
Living sweetly ~
Floating like fluffy clouds
Tenderness of our hearts ~ softer than down
Being in love ~ amidst splendors' joy
Passionate for lusts ~
Sharing of all and of this beautiful land
~ No emptiness exists~ if you are near
Flowers with their bloom ~ show colors for my soul
Waterfalls, not in sight I feel and hear their sounds
The night's stars twinkling so bright heaven being ours
The angelic songs in harmonies belonging to us
Holding our love having enchanted delights
Your tenderness of love's touch ~ I need so much
Loving you ~ so infinitely ~ as magic from above
Becoming a part of everything ~ in our own world
My passions like seasons always changing with you
Living this charm ~ next to you
I close my eyes ~ holding dear ~ love for you
As for tomorrow ~ love from you ~ is in another day

Love in Me

Genuinely think of me in seeing honest and true

How for reality in security yet marvelous of trust given

Dream in the stars let them enchant your thoughts

Feeling good in the fresh air you breathe

The intrigue of an ever-reaching sea dawning upon horizons

Casting prettiest of thoughts into your mind

Forgetting not the big, wonderful sky for hopes it holds

The soft of blue or the cloud creating changes moods to explore

Watch of flowers~ flights of birds~ soaring for freedoms living

A lovely creation growing as the other landing for making nests

These will tell you of me

The romantic moon glowing in a winds' breeze

Silhouettes casting soft shadows

Forming swaying motions of impressions for the tenderness in my heart

They are whispering in me the beauty of you with your love

Capturing my soul of the prettiness in your ways

Releasing my passions living dreams of love

Caressing your body letting you feel all my love within

For us to walk slowly holding of hands amongst beauties of this land

Always so tenderly cherishing this loveliness of you and I

Luz Estella

I peer out my window into the night

The neon clock lit mystical of relevance

The winter tree leafless waiting for life

Blue-black grayish night air appearing silent in living

So still yet picturesque revealing secrets to my mind

I think that of you then I think of love

Your wonderful sight-feel-touches so warmly magnificent

Doors opened to passageways in love

From this night's view the stories of understandings they whisper to me

How even hate answers to love yet deciding to turn away

In the silent air avid of nuance acknowledging in my brain

Channeling decisions making of certainty never turning you away

Enthusiasm in love leaving reticent for the winds blowing lost forever, ridden of the dull insensitive abounding us aflame in passion

The bliss of you in all I saw out my window, a life ready to live

Treasures unlimited in you radiating love's feelings

Precious are your gifts to cherish forever

Benevolence implanted in my wisdom continual Vowing in me giving love more enchantingly

Passion River

Oh, Passion River hear my plea

Make of me the beds in your beauty guiding, floating me along

Lending me your unwary endless streams

Granting strengths at every curve

Cooling refreshing ways soaking her heart in love with me

You the harmony's serenity please bestow your blessing upon me

Oh, Passion River generate my love real and lovely as you

That she will flow her love too me

Make me her shore where she would rest her heart

Let me be her reflections for love

Passion River mirror this harmony to me

Teach me your ways continual beauty in my soul

Tranquility all around making her heart smile for me

Passion River saturate me that she will love me just for me

Drench my passions of endless streams that will flow beautifully

Wetting her thirst for love in giving too me

Rowing on a river of love only for us

Never ceasing beauties in my passions only for her

Grant to me serenity take me along Oh Passion River

Make me flow of a love just for her and me

You would think Magical

Love's intensity covering life's intricacies
Filling completely leaving no vacancies
This touch moves reality into magical feelings
Enchanted motivating fairy tale realizations
Growing concerns in making happier
Desires magnified knowing no ending
Life's blossom the loveliest of sensations
Infinity captures you as hopes become living
Warmth's showing truths in sincerity's
Most gleeful never leaving alienated or lonely
Of sweet energy flowing shared with another
Thoughts created for gifts in sheer beauty
Visions portrayed by nature's Wonderment's
Passageways lay painted for us to see and follow
Tangibility's heaven knowing like magical so real
Simplicity's marvel bestowing feelings so mystical
Alluring joys in play and laughter spontaneously
This brought alive in realms of splendor's contentment
Radiance glowing life's happiness
Galaxie stars ignite when love finds you for another

Love's Journey

Love to most is thinking of singing within
Pulling emotions into thoughts
Battles souls from this cold cruel world
Earth's mystic in beauty helps us cling
Loveliness to see beholding for our hearts
Time and age contending against itself
Erosions from innocence purities of a child
Bruised affections taken wayside
Reality's twist for the dreams of love
How in birth when everything so small
Adorable fondles this cradle of love
In us dreams as flowers seen
Unlimited blue skies in hope passion grows
Sunlight fades cloudy stormy-gray dreariness
Unlocks treasures for compassion's felt
Opposites known livens battles for our soul
Coping in understanding with imperfection
Love born emotional becoming of wisdom
Forgetting selfish creating dreams in sharing
Charisma flows ~ now you are ready ~ for love

Hopes

Hopes - Joys - Thrills - fulfilled
Desires of possessing all of them
Forthcoming of them so much play
Wit becomes quick as a flash
Spontaneity's intellect as a garden in bloom
Imaginative impressions so effortlessly so tirelessly
Anticipation's hunger as infinite
Life in love started from a kiss
Miraculous happiness for forming another you
Ideals making better for them to live
Another chance in witnessing life
Learning more of what and how in the sharing of it too
Deep of your mind's thoughts into the soul
Life's journey past its' adventures
Making for excitement's feel yet turning meaningful
Finding resolution for and of those questions never ending
Ever so wanting to live another day
Capturing all the beauties radiantly to show its' feelings
Rewards in giving for another to join in
Portraits of life lived so picturesque by you

I am Sorry

Prominence too ethics or values help overcome imperfections

Promissory to the priorities on choices decided

Especially consistency in morals finding better ways

Rational although positive can lose too perplexities of emotions

Another route from thinking to feelings resides perpendicular

Truth lays silent so that feelings may have purity

Love's answers go challenged even to the very much in love

People's thoughts have variations yet hurt feelings linger

Never a sentence will fix abused emotions that easily

Time allotted in showers of affections softens for consideration

Like that of a high wire walker we will tread safe and sorrowful

Only to those loved we become so emotional

Too others we merely regret our misguided impoliteness

Just as an obstacle we try to correct and rightfully so

Love's joy aches so on its' avenues we do journey

Inside of love the treasures in reverence cherished

Solitude's splendor in giving of all for one to be happy

Imperfections of human the errors in judgment that can spoil totality

So, trials and tribulations we go through those hurting times

Living and learning to keep love's blossom

Page One

Your Chapter

A mind compiled like that of a book yet so unique of its' own

Being that it lives in you like anyone else who is alive

Every day of thinking and of its imaginations or in its every experience

Of my writing's I just say what you think and feel supplying meanings on paper

Readers let authors donate both of our time if written interesting

As the world is a story by simply watching

People's lives showing what living is or is not or can be about

Most know 'what' yet some know not 'how' and some not 'why'

Concrete cities cannot rejuvenate yet built amazing superficial

Explaining why politicians behave like in a school yard's playground

Exotic sensations or places created before your eyes

Earth continually amazing in endless chapters of rejuvenation

Picturesque yet fierce making one consider

Melodies in nature sometimes heard silently

Of sights it plays orchestras in your mind

Harmony flows simplicity's smoothness, though complexity understood

Your eyes see that of natural and in hearts will search for truths

Variety's change will fill senses forever never dulled

Still retains balances even fun but commitments achieving putting it all together

Rhythm for the Soul

You hear music's feel flowing becoming within

Harmonies in a feeling delightfully filling your soul

Musician artists you remember prevailing in pleasures of words or sounds

Like a something you've seen as enchantment's you invisibly touch

Feelings engulf your very soul

Seasoned with intense or simple living so happily content

Passions of beauty form vividly, enduringly consuming desires

Those visions in music so alive enlightening within

Inside soul's orchestras lay playing detailed life's entireties

Laughter, joy, excitements, appreciation's

Nothing sweeter than realizing how fortunate it is to live

Music thought in rhythms casting the stories that can be lived

Fulfilling in us dances wanted and needed for more life

In times reminisced the somberness' touch of compassion

Sharing inside for another's loss of something beautiful

Flowers in meadows along hillsides randomly colored against the skies

Red-yellow-blues the pinks and purples nature artistically spread about

Souls captured through ears and eyes form bliss through actual sounds of music

Inside yourself collected treasures of the blessings continuous of love and play

Wake Up

You know what you're thinking about
You know what you've got to lose
All your heart's dreams if you stay in a snooze
Move into your passions letting them cruise
Be ready to do what you got to do
Come on stand up believe in you
If you don't none can or will do it for you
Jump up get ready to live what you feel
Don't let your dreams lay idle in vacant fields
Knowing these words are easy to realize
Passions in you knowing this true
Your soul's heart sings in whispers to you
Don't give up by not listening to your melodies
Tap your foot believing potentials
Let your dreams fly you will soon be amazed
How to become dreams inside set free
Open your eyes starting for seeing
All the wondrous things to be
Wake up it's all yours to seize
Everything you ever wished or wanted if you try to be

A Star inside of You

Gazing at being dazing from exceptionalism stories awed
Inspirational for dreams
Thoughts splendid in splendor
So imaginative of real
Desires for living coming more alive
Inside your soul springs and clings to life
Visions of those carrying dreams along living them out
Guides for yours in possibilities for yours coming true
Sides of doing, creating or recipient
Inspiration in admiration but not inferior are you
A decision you think
Yet dreaming wishes the portraits in your mind
Passions for living in being, as seen, thought, and felt
Yet artists feel into feelings attached with those of your own
Letting you become in journeys accompanied by them
The companion you need, besides that of love
The silence in you whispers then sings, excitingly! Fulfilling!
Whether you can share, or it finds you
Alone never will you be! Others are like you.

Heart and Soul

Life's joys shown majestically with sensations in simple smiles
Feeling magnifications so magnificently adventurous thrills
Spontaneity's creating living lively too enjoy
Alluring enchantments bestowed a loose in fun's pleasure
Laughter's tribute giving the physical happiness enriching moods
Love's depth is there for us in stability of realizations
So precious this gift of life
Starry nights cast the infinite galaxies of other realms intriguing
Thought's imagination's never endless
Reality showing common ground
Sorrow amplifies love's tenderness
Making love is nature's gift also to have
Giving or receiving so breathtaking
In the soul everlasting belonging to you
Childlike plays of innocent endeavors still grasped
Even the incredibly old can touch this blessing
Mentalities too ponder
Existence in modern societies
A world of intrigue for conversation
But what is inside a person lay the original rainbow's mystic

Of You

Once upon a time the depths of your mind

Conclusions to dreams sprang vividly alive

Hopes for life being content with elaborate imaginations

Dreams in subtleties or beauties to dynamic adventurous excitement

Vast emotions so revealingly rewarding as you walk

In dreams the enrichment of desires for lives and life's endeavors

Believing the will of loveliness although one must enact

Yet of these dreams so alive in most everyone

How wonderful to dream on your own possibilities to share amongst

The affect has an effect that softens anxieties for anyone

Laying down compassion's touch that we all need at times

All the groundwork in place leaving for extravaganza's ideals

Theatrically enduring with intelligence or wit

Portrayals of gallantry so noble or the flights of the rich

Meek and sweet also to the simple ideas of living

Enjoying the sweet smells and sights of nature or walking downtown

Becoming of all yet somber to the imperfections not so pretty

Well-balanced personalities come included with thoughts and feelings

Naturalism of earth yet human in desires to flirtatiously accept life

Never an excuse to be bored or plunder life away.

Reserved

Centered to the essence in him or her
Some will hide in reserve inwardly for themselves
So quiet in formed reverence making you think
Non-boisterous resonating yet showing concern's virtue
Provision with precision contemplated before spoken
Concrete aftermath's not losing respect
Machinery well-oiled smoothly the pistons up and down
Understandings progress teaching to be better
Yet are maze's in maintaining focus of well balanced
When-when not-not what-but how~ makes quite the difference
Styles a trickery in what appears of acceptance
Imperfections considered as very few periods can be placed as absolute
Formatting IN's and Out's - the How and the Why to consider
Sailboats without rudders aimlessly drifting amidst winds and currents
This could be you if not maintaining your essence
Within is a voice of reason if you will listen
Uncanny yet as real in phenomenal as all of nature's presence
Inside you the potentials to become as beautifully balanced
Enchantingly enhanced mystical allure
We the tools to nature's bliss genuine abilities of magnificence

Tic thinking Toc feeling

I see things that I don't know much about

Listening to things that I don't quite understand

Yet I feel things showing me more of why

Expressions may lose but a feeling is hard to stop ~DE Vinci might know

Things seeming complex only needing an ally

Invisible seventh sense the emotion of feelings consisting in thought

Knowing without completely understanding

Feelings take you in other directions, but both find a path

The strongest companion engulfing all of you

Mystic infatuation's affection from thinking

Overwhelmed moments in laughter or if tears fallen

Magic to living but reality's negligence

Thinking creates astounding possibilities

Yet feelings touch inside everyone's soul

Connections to yourself as for others to know

Attraction's knowledge goes beyond

Like a relationship thinking and feeling they need of the other

No person lives without these two companions

Not a person has said the combination is always easy

Poetry

The words in thoughts for feelings within
Descriptive ideas spoken visionary painting of a mind
Colorful imprints of tangibility in mentality too see and taste
Softness in the gentle warmth's linking subdued strengths
Love's affections in true feelings for endearments to keep
Continual essence already there just radiating life's harmony
Planted in nature's impressions she is being the artist
She dawned earth in lovely colors enchanted
Energies astonished that amaze one forever
All her beauties yet still portraying fierce
Teacher of psychology enforcer of balances
Before our eyes witnessing the good and bad
Appreciation's she guides in you to understand
As a poet bearing insights for seeing our capabilities bestowed
Road maps to follow showing natural of living
What she gives in infinite realizations
Tutorial every day the visions in thoughts she also creates
A paradise and reality for all living amongst her
Beauties cast for love's freedoms in us intelligently play

Prognostication

Rainy-wet-soggy days for filling mellow feeling's

Maybe dreary in sights although surprisingly refreshing

Reflections of life mirrored like forecasts

One must feel or think too be able to create

Not for sleep but thoughts as dreams capture reality

Self-esteem's aspiring radiance knowing not just an atom creates

Energy's intellect shadowing activity

Watching how the world becomes slowed from a rain

Moments to absorb more of the life around

Feelings of soft too intense as you reflect

Stored in you the things to live and give back

Impressions of sights and thoughts

Replete in voracious ideas within

Yours to liven a dreary day

To become with time in slow relaxed modes

Listening with ease learning of another

Weather perfect for conversation

Seeing how even laughter is found least expected

If alone the paradox of all this is still yours

Reflecting spawns' cognition

Eased Intentions Unlimited

Laughing for opening doors too and for minds
Playing adds wanting company in making more
Oh, how seeing makes you want to talk
Silence only intensifies beauty's ideas
Of energetic fun and playful energy coming alive
Combining harmonies in smooth transitions like day and night
Flowing as a breeze or whirling as the winds
Charisma shown the same blue as the sky can be
Your presence upon others this they do see
Smile's casual influence radiates even a small conversation
Sureness' foundations in balances for astounding searches
Lighthearted ease becoming deep into thoughts
Not all answers yet closer in understanding
Growing in steps planting self-confidence
Gifts inherited searching for living in truths
Solidarity forms like a guiding light
Beacons in you attract other's attentions
All the while your being attracted too
The polish for clarity adorned in you shines
Without hope's glimmer humanity forever goes dark inside

Mingled Acquaintance

In times when people exchange in mentalities

Some seem like arithmetic some like algebra

Awareness like geometry some ahead in trigonometry's

Extraversion's excursions into possibilities but back to mathematical

Feelings of compassion motivate yet some are just for comfort

Giving of oneself beneficially hoping to further any formula along

Differences of giving and taking while thinking in patience's virtue

Love of being-

Love of alive-

Love of humanity

Loving in a relationship

Thinking sacrifice of self and time

Passions...

Many things of intensities including lusts

Yet love is the best to have it with for all the right balances

Controversy is putting faith in a relationship abstract as trigonometry

Alone seems easier and mentally achievable

Although haunted by the word love

Sharing of love's stability is undeniably worthwhile

Somehow roots too whatever thoughts pass by

Resuming of the mingle almost quaint in abiding time

Unleashed

If not for childhood humanity imprisoned more from feelings
Innocence remained has kept compassion
Although good prevails yet bad or evil goes untamed
Why the humankind spins around in confusion
While natures' earth created complete and revealing even self-sustained
Mankind still thinks materialistically as not so true of the Indian
If humanity's soul were the concentration
Things of now would be more fulfilling
Not the high-priced concepts of money and the ideals of power
Abolishing in the lies to betrayals of some people and politicians
If true with the morals of living and the power were compassionate
Greed would become second to those fringes of materialistic
Understandably reality teaches survival as so true with nature
Protections of freedoms for ridding dangers saving self-preservations
Close to the weed in the garden that overtakes beauty
Yet why this dream of peace so desired internationally
Earth given free and the world thinks of domination
Societies built mostly in superficial architectural gratification
Imperfections yet meek and humble have no agenda
Granting spiritual as well with naturalism leads too recognition's

Painted Idea's

Expectations arise because we love and so love to live
Reality to some will not allow even dreams
Life's sensations along with nature's wonderland
Stability of blessings shown simply in a sunrise's sunset
Enchantment alive casting silhouettes for more
Becoming in us fun's imagination
Centered or along edges of outer realms
In some minds creating superficial
Balances we must know or victims we become
Choices in direction at our will and whim
Focus never should we lose being able to see through
Fad or style caused metropolitan minds
Caught in the whirl of mankind's self-made
Oblivious for nature's natural allure
Love even sex take different shapes
Victims of superficial have not any sacred realm
Boundaries fade casting only a maze
Discontent makes followers of the weak
Superficial always needs new dose's
Natural is blessed of stability's contentment sharing balances of the two.

Playgrounds & Disciplines

Watching of life and the living of it is seen through people
Good or bad a noticeable main difference
Destitute one's showing needs for compassion
Some successful one's not exceedingly flowing in compassion
Ego's flare yet of the meek it glows
Yet destitute always paints humanity's hope
The eagle so proud yet help their own
With watchful eye they protect, giving of food
Oh, how we can learn if we listen
As horses sense danger before it even happens
A grand warning provided for all around
Then the dogs so loyal no matter their treatment
Life amongst us are guides so rewardable for us in gains
Reaping benefits for harmony coming alive
Just as the blue sky in sunshine enlightens a smile
Pretty sights given for enjoyments' thriving
Yet the storms and of deaths making us realize
Liffe a precious gift for us being in respected reverence
Joys alive yet griefs for bearing demonstrates how life is
One life to live best becoming in the balance of how to do it right

Reality

If in pleasant views your eyes so filled with delights
Absorbed of appreciation the mentality is pondering thoughts
Easily imagined the peace and harmony including love
Not so smooth this transaction compares in the ways of the world
Revolutionary ideas as people strive to change and hopefully not self-served
Solidarity for humanity should be concerns for common existence
Generosity for the necessities for the needy but are not given to ones not
A poor person offers a smile giving of his possessions
Most rich hesitate only smiling when possessions gained
Born the same with blood but separate ideas personally
Besides the good or bad some wish to rule their opinions
Nations of society form idealistic views, yet some dictated
Governed in laws protecting justice, other things powered by money collected
Minuet given back appearing humanistic, yet some elected ones live royally
Civilization needs correcting not governed by aristocratic opinion
Freedoms the equality in thinking more successful but far from better
Governments live off people but soon their corruption prevails
Soon policies written might as well be for cattle and not so much for people
Ideas become enforced containing freedom one size fits all for their convenience

The World that Is not

Raindrops

Clouds mysteriously mystic

Kissing lips ~ tender hearts

Gleefully playing of laughter

Star-filled skies ~ twinkling in the night

Thoughts too Angelic feelings

Gifts from life

Thoughts merged becoming one in love

Sunlight for all the living

Breathe of life's Blessings ~ bestowed upon you and I

Wondrous ~ pretty sights ~ nature's enchanting inspiration

Earth in context so perfectly balanced

Dreams~ Love~ Harmony and Peace~ Imagination~ Playing~

All the tools are given for thinking

But the reality governed by the nations in our world sure is not

In You

Reminiscing times that are afar

Yesterday's wishes of things that slipped away

Intuition spoke yet you so failed in listening

Daydreaming brings into focuses of attention

And your wish is this to be perfect now

When so young and moving so fast

Easier fooled that some things can be had later

What's right what is wrong is really known

Just inclinations wishing for it to work out on its' own

Obliged information you say shrugging off misfortune

The saying of history repeating itself are your ears listening now

Uncanny sensations instinctively intuition that inner voice

Feels as if gambling for its' not a sure shot but it is called exertion

So, how many times we do not believe in ourselves for something

Looking for that solid situation staring you square in the face

Keep wishing you might be

ancient before it happens

Earth's magic of nature especially mystic whispers for you to listen

This creation's amazing beauties in phenomenal capabilities

Hot melts with an ease then we should understand

Earth's energy all around even in us to be attuned to intuition

Progress

If you ever did wonder about the why of existence
Seeing life's creations believing it true
You will look within pausing to be as real
This modern era's pace takes away from natural
Plastic in a stretched imagination replaced values
Existence formed in materialistic desires
Feelings paused for survival as people made it that way
In soul's wish the innocent babe's birth following too young
Thoughts of now knowing without dollars you fade away
Soon beauties are not seen just dreamt dreams
Existence becomes routine yet nature blooms
Modernism submits struggles for you to stay ahead
Plans from childhood we will work hard to achieve
Materialistically thought to live lovely as a tree
Lost will some become falling aside just in hopes
Monetary appears to be the only solution
This planet created as a garden for us to be productive not idle
Humanity learned the wrong directions
Now exists turmoil, protection, the costs of survival
So, after the beginning of civilization progress is life, in spent dollars

Seeds Planted

Loud crashes of thunder ~ streaks of lighting
Inside stirring feelings of fright
Hopes lingering in focus not to be harmed
Security clinging questioning protections
Nature's directions in using hope with intelligence
People soon forget concluding knowing it all
Morality becomes mentality not even spiritual
The troubled misguided paths for society
This earth of scientist's state evolved
Yet earth did not use science ~ it created it
In all its' beauties creating even included rejuvenation
We are the most special of all
Yet some believe they the heads of it all
Give to those who do not have to obtain
Watch the lack of concerns in handling
If not for emotion the secret seventh sense
Uncanny sensations guiding in leading to total truths
Logical would only leave not any beauties to feel
Bestowed in us is the secrets from nature

Survival's Friend

Miles put distances as time needs nurturing
Absence deals with the heart and a mind missing it
Realizing like a ladder climbing learning life's lessons
Living is balanced with thought and emotion
You are as the wizard and juggler making better
No matter whatever has and will happen
Inside you this will for living kept alive
Examples of others or scholars for guides
Your soul always will whisper directions to follow
Looking amongst differences finding beautiful differs as flowers
We are too also of the same plan this part of nature
No denial's life's the most marvelous of all
The choosers are we yet sometimes followers we must be
Knowing amazing capability life inspires as teaches
The passions and fun thrill you as a smile waiting to spring
Melancholy's solemn appreciation, but joys gleefully open them
Inside volumes of thoughts fill your mind posing as encyclopedias
Feelings beyond philosophy's psychology always growing
We are destined to live, laugh, and learn
Hope and love are in our second name

Pondering

Controversy is such a big word it tells on itself

People's thoughts cannot always put periods behind ideas

Only thing good about bad is knowing the mistake

Free will the choice not in chains

Few times does perfection come from thin air

Things created by this are realizations

Rise of spiritual~ simple in lovely thoughts~ visions to love of life

God is perfect especially for church, yet religion might have detours for God's path

Man creates~ not so funny or strange how he learned of this hint, hint

Trouble sprouted believing people the gods~ forming crooked lead ways

Life a big word due to its' Creations~ everybody accepts of this

Love everyone does believe in and knows it is ageless

Laughter is something everybody desires~ shares and feels

But to tell you how to live this is not a clever idea

Creation again shows you we all have our own way

Trouble pops up as some have different or possible warped sense of ideas

People have not perfected in their ways

Looking at earth making perfect as it makes up its' mistakes

And how do we know it is a mistake when balances cover its' existence

Wonder why God is a hard to accept He even gives free choice

Passageways

Uncanny the more we are alike the more differences we find
As merry-go-rounds back to the beginning
Individualism's logic too scholar intellect
Humanity's specialty of unique
Common too magicians we create
Secrets learned realizing changes are not for shallow opinions
Playfully as children skip in frolicking, mentality accepts challenges
Adults' trick in keeping energized with intellect's freedom's
Correlation's exercise we share establishing connections
Preserved ideas in examples of liking yet not buying
Intricate views due to complexities of more than one idea
Intellectual acceptance even if we prefer another angle or way
Before us lies the phenomenal in wonderful beauties of nature
Steppingstones for infinite realizations through our eyes to the mind
Outlines shown in recognizing ultimate possibilities
Sailors we cruise adventurously desiring truths
Intrigues as scholars are we to learn of living
Happiness gained through freeing of our soul
Pastures and seas filling skies gaining more knowledge
Energies factual reflecting continual after death considering amazing life

Mine or Yours

Wondering is truly destined for discovery
Considering possibilities
Infinite thoughts about this way or the other
Lost at times in never-never land it seems
These are funny as they get silly
Then in a flash the mind swerves drastically in turns
This survival of mentality coming back into focus
Learning lessons from misguided trends of thinking
Fortunate of less or bad for it teaches of more and better
Gained tendencies taught from errors and trials
Self-induced methods from the subconscious
Silently composed invisibly though created by our mind
Self-correcting built-in protectors of thinking
Calculating of more probably as fast as Superman
Trying to find conclusions of a thought
Yet finding more solutions to keep on thinking
How, when, when not, not how but why compiling like that of geometry
Interestingly intriguing finding so much to imagine
Almost carried away from the original contemplation
Now the concentration sharpened to solve thoughts

Inspirations of Play

If we were to think of life with no range
What a dead-end street we could create
If acceptance were only in the living and of dying
Then why those desires to live anyway
Still remains that essence of how it can be
For if it were not, we would be already dead inside
As winds rustle leaves or ripples the water
Spirited in us joys and ideas to be happy
Spontaneity of fun is one of the reasons we stay alive
Not only material of riches that enables
For the mind needs only the thoughts to imagine
The visions of play always make us smile
Either mental or physical goes hand in hand
But with not the insights to distinguish
We become lost in an imbalance roaming with dissatisfaction
Who never smiled at the child who played with nothing?
Thoughts in truth that all we need is guidance in ourselves
Realizing the concept of sharing expands ever so much more
Now, we become with life ready to give back its' beauty

Universal

What if there were no earth?
Just a spaceship in the universe
No concepts of flowers in a meadows range
Minus the colors and trees against blue or gray skies
Not anything of beauty or pretty in sight
No feel for breezes so cool and refresh
Just the scientific culture for happiness
Wonder if people would be more of a robotics mind?
Just the calculated factual precise in thoughts
Compassion hopefully should still be intact
Passions of love hopefully would still be there
Excitements in adventure as planets zoomed by
But most everything even earth one of a kind
I think the stars would save us humans
Plenty of room for starry enchanting of beauty's births.
Just how different we might be without any earth?
Life has miraculous gifts we would still go on.
Living creates the most beautiful desires where imagination thrives.
We would be not much different for life has its' surprise!
Humans would still be the intrigue of unique

Entity

Gazing up into the air letting imaginations fly

Looking at airports wondering about other places

Desires mount possibilities

Emotions grow wanting life to be amazingly more

Variations of different sights places with memories

The wind's taste for knowing you are not idle

Cultures differ yet humanity the denominator

Good, bad, or different will people be as coins having opposite sides

The world for you to explore

Rich or poor does not really matter

Experiencing is priceless

Inspirations' views' fill your mind

Realizing knowledges gained

Capabilities' marvel in your physical body's sensation's

A little shallower sat alongside meanings of life

Even the world's portrayal with its' civilization's

Casting sights of earth's beauties inspired thoughts within

As if we are here to experience then afterwards soaring

A wonderful stage in learning righteous as life's more than seen

The possibility too where life will go

One plus Two Equals

Uncanny the miracle astounded of things born gifted with life

No matter of what seed the species allowing growth

Not surprisingly the foods of substance on earth provided

No matter what life needed to sustain it was granted

Even beforehand with trees creating oxygen

As for us giving too them their elements needed

What an organized plan intricately devised masterminded at will

Earth to be life granting more life in these continuing cycles

Not a vivid imagination must you have to understand

We humans blessed with the most delighted enlightened blessing

Automatically we smile when happy frown of sad and laughter shakes our body

Newborn babes demonstrate innocence as people's mentality expands continually

Thoughts come to us as if whispered on winds

Feelings engulf our passions bestowing insight for gaining knowledge

Driven by this life created inside instinctively we journey

Evolving from the beginning this creation deliberately cast

Knowing more is about you than just your mind and heart… It is your soul

Things non-mechanical if you will~ already bestowed that really makes for living

A soul knows~ but the mind does not easily accept to understand

Twilight Zone's Nonfiction

Observations about animals at play thinking our similarities exists

Intelligence no matter how small points significantly living is amazing

Instincts shown is what makes this living coexistent

Plants a marvel for us in another consciousness of existence

Their beauties so intricate we are lost in explanations

Expectancy we have grown concluding as merely decorative

Sitting in forests watching all these things of unity each a plan

Humanity the head yet seemingly more the other domain coincides

From them we see of us consequently learning more from life

Yet energies beyond all this proves living is minor compared to this Creation

The atmospheres even planets far out into other galaxies

Phenomenal experiences in other dimensions

Of older times the wizardry practiced proved mind can beat matter

Many things of existence are past realities in common normalizes

Of this life realizing what is seen thought and felt are passageways

The conception of thinking goes beyond our body's physical

Ideas in awareness from us comes in messages we did not create

Inspirations are the winds flowing for us to catch

Normality's peacefully explanation of tranquility in rest

Genius's fine line of insanity yet histories of phenomenal exists

Nonfictions

Wizard-hat-crystal-ball-mystical night's stars shinning bright

Moon's glow laid silhouettes' softly across terrain's

Black nights turned visually of enchanted portraits for viewing

Waterfalls sounding thunderous into pretty ponds filled of Lilly's

Rocks and flowers laid in forests with greenery all about

Swooping birds making sounds of play as turtles and fish's swim

Pretty white clouds dawned across an eternal blue sky

Butterfly's beauty masterminded of harmony's innocent purity

Winds singing softly moving through the air

Sun lit rays casting golden light yet warmth's for playing

Morning dews as earth's coffee offering all its inhabitants

Raindrops fulfilling every thirst

Serenity's tranquility granted these paradise settings

Howling storms formed from intensity's beauty

Spawning hungers of every kind for the beauty was ignored

Downfalls of perfection starting imperfections existing

Eating of the appealing

Danger is now amidst

Out of the forests into the cities

Death or greed common as nature's thunderstorm and we did not listen

Willpower

You can take a perspective thought

Then look at a rock

Seems like taking of air creating physical

Combining the two for solid lines in thinking

Forming a trend for logic as imaginations rationalization follows

Matters not in the limited frames of ordinary

If you mastered solidarity

Abstract in thoughts though concrete in search of meanings

Mind expansion knows not limitation, yet boundaries exist

The energy has started, and you must follow intelligently

Logic leads to truths, but the truth is always of its' own

Non bendable ~ unbreakable ~ it stands alone even with honor

Truth stayed remaining the same through the ages during the time of all era's

More of truth is found through time as thoughts lead us there

That rock and thought in the air are bridging gaps for us to understand

Nothing complete in life unless we admit to the Wonderment

Some thoughts for the impaired but senses are heightened

Still, you cannot dispute the blessings for life created

For the best balance to life is from the soul

Logical in dreams enlightened with Wonderment and always remember too play

Why

I look to the stars
Remember my childlike ways
The days of play
Innocent ways
Those stars disappear with the dawning of the sun…
Hope lingers, for yesterday is gone
A gift so pure as this life to live…
Why does innocence have to be plundered
The joys and hopes to seem only to be in a dream…
What a mistake was made after life began
As reality will unfold the toil in our existence…
At least we have the heart feeling splendor
All the learning aiding in hopes…
That life was to be of play and innocence
Maybe when it is through…
We can live the splendor.
Dancing with the joys, in play and laughter.

What Happened

Breath of air though sometimes being not so pleasant

People in treatment too others' we capture realizing the same

Consideration changes ill effects

Cleaning out does for wonders refreshing your surroundings

Imperfection ~ yes but not for the lack of improving

I must have been born of a different mold

Emphasis on self-importance voids other's existence

Of society states reliant on others shrugging off individual

Yet heard a village to raise children

Confusion due too superficial concern not seeing past ones' own face

Schools given accomplishing tools in how to think hopefully not what to think

Newer generations in general speaking are more of self-concern

Witness degeneration of complaisance in courtesy and morals

The sky the limit is fun and for unleashed opportunities

Not for unlimiting the disciplines or lack of self-control

The golden rule forgotten these past generations

Do unto others as you would have them do unto you

Wild West's we tamed only now to repeat ill-mannered

Segregation is won, true and of good~ now is spun self-concern

Our society spiraling out of control ~ backwards makes no difference

Tuning Knobs Inwardly

Out of eyes becoming as personal windows

Scenery illuminates of those peered wonders into thoughts

As others looking on the inside see a glimpse of you

Sometimes almost troublesome they can be hindered and obscured

Bewildering behaviors portraying self-centered

Conscienceless of others unless thinking of their own noses

Frustration's mount yet wisdoms know a kindness soothes

Understandings take up the slack for lack of better

Back to your 'window' soaking pleasantries views

Only closing them to debris or the sights of those lacking decency

Procedure's preservations even carried over into your thoughts

Mirrors as reflections so do not be ugly with your ways

Protection's exceptions reserved only for survival

Electric switched on or off cliché' for walking away

Barren desert's void's yet beyond is a mountainous range

Things of substance keeps loveliness' in focus for hope

Energies created envisioning harmonies well and alive

Inside you like a sea's stretch touching the sky

Enchanted enlightenments for angelic moments

Choices for blossoming lovely or as a weed unsightly

Ways

Compassion with cares for feeling tenderness

Living the beauty, portrayed in earth's garden of nature

Transposing this into daily lives for others we would make smile

No more aggravations passing along so rudely for others to feel

If we just were as our eyes seeing enchantment

The emotions in feeling delights from sights of beauties

Our soul grows lovely for living so alive with passions

Yet our poor minds so filled with realities and dismays

Hard to distinguish at times wanting the compassionate way

Intrigues we always recognize or desired fun for play

How amazing the physical body

Our mind has many capacities venturing out and in upon

Even the will to calm dangers or those dismays

Channeling of thoughts being concerned

Figuring out the best possible outcomes embracing all of life

Simply putting our hearts and soul into the feelings of living

Applying them with our thoughts to be of and do

Like clouds in a sky roaming off somewhere

As rain in creating replenishment's

Fantastic if we become proof that concerned is passionate of living

Fused Confusion and Non

In times with people
They are in arithmetic
I am in Algebra
My conscience aware of geometry
Then again, some so ahead with trigonometry
Views so different might as well use mathematical descriptions
On the prospect of feelings and compassion—-
Some are self-centered or just empty
Of ones giving not shallowed of selfish but concerned benefits for all around
The difference of giving and taking
Love—-love of being-love of humanity
Love in a relationship
Thinking sacrifice of self and time
Passions~ Many things of intensities and lusts
Yet love is the best to have it with
Not a controversy—-mixing all which is good
Putting too faith in a relationship has one thinking
Alone~ Seems easier and mentally achievable
Though haunted by the word love
Sharing is the ultimate for the best even just helping people

Negligence

Natural orders to the things such as coexistence

Regrets to those negligent for this procedure to be forgotten

Perceptions being that society accepts an orchestrated functional

Nature's unfailing balance made precise its' harmony

Society altars for fitting opinions too accommodations

If all were born as adults, this might prevail yet there are children

Naive of youth being susceptible one would think society would mentor

Now the order of and too things become incredibly significant

Sheltering children from the misguided zealous

Immaturity uses his or her decisions especially if sexuality

Bestowed upon a child who knows little of living

Opinionated adults make crisscrossed interpretations

Principles have basics to whatever implied circumstantial or situation

Nurturing is practiced for infants as mentors should be for children

Modern times of now are fast omitting the child's innocence

We created our public agendas, yet society exploits humankind

Leaving no time to grow children wise naturally into life's arena

Right or wrong unquestioned lessens gatherings of knowledge

Culturally a mistake of overlooking the natural order of living

Yet this goes on and cries ring out in misguided youths.

Life Abused

A man at war loses
Purity of innocence learning many aggressions
Inside torn his ideals again for beauty
Weaknesses he no longer can afford
Laughter depleted— only coldness not joy
All essences of loveliness- playful lost- becomes just a memory
For survival instinctively driven he must cling
The dark sides of humanity he witnesses trying not to become
Yet honor should never be gone in him to keep no matter what
Adjacent to himself casting aside feelings
Only winning and living especially living are on his mind
In a struggle for existence instinctively emotionless—he will end another's life
Human existence is surviving and only for his soldiers he tries to smile
Politically stanched for good or for principles he chose a side
Deep in his soul growing many scars
Relentless dreams in nightmare or crazy mixed-up things
Not wanting to lose inside—his preexistence living life before
Where the word beauty only casts hope
For its' feeling so long lost in another world
His only concern and main wish that it all was not in vain

Rightfully So

Nine Eleven Two Thousand One
Remorse and anger of the innocent abused
Avenge flowed in our blood
Justification rightfully so
Abolishment of evil we all knew
Killing those who killed thousands of us
Foreign lands imposing death on us
War cried in our voice
Off to fight to make right but when we got back
Open all doors to finish the fight as corruption is a form of evil
On our streets in halls of justice
Our shores let to be contaminated
If we could take the full step
Abolishing of bad and evil
Passing judgment and condemning the guilty
Making a true society prevailing in good
Nine Eleven Two Thousand One A landmark for stopping all bad
Mindset started accepting no corruption
Terrorists-thieves even corporate or judicial even thugs
Dungeons even graveyards determined for all the guilty

Wishing

The sky being upwards helps lifts our hopes

Enlightened mystic flows from the stars

Looking down filled from seeing amazements making us humble

Far away gives time to think

Around the bend heightens imaginations' expectations

Getting lost makes respect for having directions

Death's contemplation's preserves reverence

Hope is our love in dreams awake

Someone gazed upwards giving birth

Planted humanities distanced around all through time

Cycles of humanity instinctively bestowed

Since the beginning this life enchants

Outward of within giving freedoms even for thoughts

Pain is the taste of a bad reality

Lovely views sights or emotion develop in us beauty

Lands filled of trees and flowers all for the living

Pretty for us in rain ~ sunshine or winds

Storms and cruelties from nature and humankind

Why this maze when perfection is so close

Dreams, wishes, commitments we make for believing heaven after earth

Soul

Delighted from the merriment of glee~ soaring in realms of fun

Highlighted spontaneous rushing sensations for playing in laughter

Thrilling being alive over-flowing with excitement and wit

The eyes fill minds with positive splendid visions

Like the rubbing from legs of crickets singing harmonies too your soul

All of nature with lovely awes absorbing splendors of amazement

Springing upwards of joy like legs from a grasshopper

Reaching atmospheres where angels should be

Floating as clouds or upon flowers on soft waved waters

Inside yourself these feelings so free and contented

Unabridged capabilities to be of and about yourself

Glowing magically iridescently attracting thoughts of others

Charisma as magnetism is to the art of living being simply happy

Free willed in optimism sharing joys to see and feel

Casting aside dreary ideas of newspapers in realities we are plagued with

Think to the flights of birds flying freely about

Let the anchors go of your mind as ships sailing out to sea

Imagine thrills and fun in the adventures for you to become

Envision the loveliest of feelings and be of these

There is always time in being deeply concerned, later

Play as a Child

Emotionally drained intellectually spent
Silence fought but never defeated
Overwhelmed with feelings where thoughts abound
Grasped by this vastness of life
Of livings' maze searching for paths or glimpses of light
Its' shine for joy of thinking to smile
Like clouds floating, creating somber yet enchanted dreams
So, of darker ones give mystical gloom
Caught in whirlwinds of passions
Intensity of desires beckoning yet not ringing
Lost where moments feel become dark
Dulled senses trying to take their flight
Remembrances of heart's soul seeking happiness
But the mind hesitates to see all reality's intersections too thoughts and feelings
Crazy desperate funny clichés' of captains and kings
Winning knowing losing is a part too
Struggles at times keeping your shine
Without a mind and heart, a soul never shows to see knowing its' truths

www.ingramcontent.com/pod-product-compliance
Lightning Source LLC
Chambersburg PA
CBHW071500070526
44578CB00001B/401